General Assembly
Distinguished Lectures
Kampala, 2002

Samir Amin
Mahmood Mamdani
Fatou Sow

Texts of the Cheikh Anta Diop, Claude Ake and Léopold Sédar Senghor lectures delivered at the CODESRIA 10th General Assembly held in Kampala, Uganda in December 2002.

Monograph Series

The CODESRIA Monograph Series is published to stimulate debate, comments, and further research on the subjects covered. The Series will serve as a forum for works based on the findings of original research, which however are too long for academic journals but not long enough to be published as books, and which deserve to be accessible to the research community in Africa and elsewhere. Such works may be case studies, theoretical debates or both, but they incorporate significant findings, analyses, and critical evaluations of the current literature on the subjects in question.

Typesetting by Hadijatou Sy-Sané

Printed by Lightning Source

CODESRIA Monograph Series

ISBN 2-86978-149-0

CODESRIA would like to express its gratitude to African Governments, the Swedish Development Co-operation Agency (SIDA/SAREC), the International Development Research Centre (IDRC), OXFAM GB/I, the MacArthur Foundation, the Carnegie Corporation, the Norwegian Ministry of Foreign Affairs, the Danish Agency for International Development (DANIDA), the French Ministry of Cooperation, the Ford Foundation, the United Nations Development Programme (UNDP), the Rockefeller Foundation, the Prince Claus Fund and the Government of Senegal for support of its research, publication and training activities.

Contents

Notes on the authors

Samir Amin is a leading political economist in the field of development studies. He is currently the director of the Third World Forum. Amin teaches economics at the Universities of Poitiers, Paris and Dakar. He has published numerous treatises on law, civil society, socialism, colonialism and development particularly in Africa and the Arab and Islamic Worlds. His numerous books include *Accumulation on a World Scale, Unequal Development, The Future of Maoism, Eurocentrism, Empire of Chaos, Re-Reading the Postwar Period* and *Spectres of Capitalism*.

Mahmood Mamdani is from Kampala, Uganda. He has taught at the University of Dar-es-Salaam, Makerere University and University of Cape Town, and is currently Herbert Lehman Professor of Government and director of the Institute of African Studies at Columbia University in New York. His previous book *Citizen and Subject: Contemporary Africa and the Legacy of Late Colonialism* was recognized as 'one of Africa's 100 best books of the 20th century' and was also awarded the Herskovitz Prize of the African Studies Association of USA for 'the best book on Africa published in the English language in 1996'. Mahmood Mamdani was President of CODESRIA from 1999 to 2002. In 2001, he presented one of the nine papers at the Nobel Peace Prize Centennial Symposium.

Fatou Sow is a Senegalese sociologist, researcher at the Centre National de la Recherche Scientifique in France. She is a professor at the Department of Social Sciences of the Institut fondamental d'Afrique noire/Cheikh Anta Diop (IFAN), Cheikh Anta Diop University (Senegal) where she also lectures on gender and development issues in the Faculty of Arts. Her publications are on development issues. She is mostly interested in African women and gender relations within African economies and cultures.

1

The Alternative to the Neoliberal System of Globalization and Militarism

Imperialism Today and the Hegemonic Offensive of the United States

Samir Amin

The Alternative: Social Progress, Democratization, and Negotiated Interdependence

What people need today, as well as yesterday, are society-wide projects (national and/or regional) articulated to regulate and negotiate globalized structures (while assuring a relative complementarity between them), which would simultaneously permit advances in three directions:

a) Social Progress: demands that economic progress (innovation, advances in productivity, the eventual expansion of the market) are necessarily accompanied by social benefits for all (by guaranteeing employment, social integration, reduction in inequalities, etc.).

b) The democratization of society in all dimensions, understood as a never-ending process and not as a 'blue print', defined once and for all. Democratization demands that its reach is felt in social and economic spheres, and not to be restricted to just the political sphere.

c) The affirmation of society-wide economic and social development, and the building of forms of globalization that offer this possibility. It needs to be understood that the unavoidable autocentric character of development does not exclude either the opening (on condition that it remains controlled) or the participation in 'globalization' ('inter-dependence'). But it conceives of these as needing to be formulated in terms that would permit the reduction — not the accentuation — of the inequalities of wealth and power between nations and regions.

The 'alternative' that we are defining by advances in three directions demands that all three progress in parallel. The experiences of modern history, which were founded on the absolute priority of 'National independence' whether accompanied by social progress, or even sacrificing it, but always without democratization, continually demonstrate their inability to go beyond the rapidly attained historical limits. As a complementary counterpoint, contemporary democracy projects, which have accepted to sacrifice social progress and autonomy for globalized interdependence, have not contributed to reinforcing the emancipatory potential of democracy, but have, instead, eroded it — even to discredit and finally delegitimize it. If, as the predominant neoliberal discourse pretends, submitting to the demands of the market presents no other alternative, and if, this idea would by itself produce social progress (which is not true), why bother voting? Elected governments become superfluous decorations, since 'change' (a succession of different heads who all do the same thing) is substituted to alternative choices by which democracy is defined. The reaffirmation of politics and the culture of citizenship define the very possibility of a necessary alternative to democratic decadence.

It is therefore necessary to advance in the three dimensions of the alternative, each one connected to the other. Less can be more — developing step-by-step strategies which allow for the consolidation of progress, even ones that are so modest that they can be achieved immediately, to go even further while minimizing the risk of failure, going off-course or moving backwards.

Making this step-by-step strategy concrete means taking into account the evolution of science and technology and the acceleration of the revolutions it has brought (and this in all its dimensions — new riches, potential destructive forces brought on by these revolutions, transformations in the organization of the workplace and social structures, etc.). But to do it, we would need not to submit, in the vain hope that these revolutions would have the 'magic' ability to by themselves resolve the challenges of social progress and democratization. It is the opposite in integrating the 'new' in a mastered social dynamic that we can exploit their eventual emancipatory potential.

The social project abusively qualified as liberal (and in its extreme form — neoliberal) is founded on the sacrifice of social progress to the unilateral demands of the short-term profits of dominant segments of capital (the transnational capital of the 500 or 5,000 largest transnational companies). Through this unilateral submission of workers, human beings, nations, to the logic of the market, is expressed, without a doubt, the permanent utopia of capital (according to which all aspects of life need to adapt to the demands of profit-making), in many ways an infantile utopia, without any scientific or ethical base. It is through this submission that social progress and democracy have been emptied of any reality.

On the global scale, this submission can only reproduce and deepen the inequalities between nations and regions, especially considering the new structures that conform to the demands of capital which has reached a new level of development. This means that 'monopolies' (sometimes known as comparative advantages) to which the oligopolies from the dominant centers (the triad) benefit, is no longer simply about industry, but also about other forms of economic, social and political control (the control of technology, reinforced by abusive practices of industrial and intellectual property, the access to the planet's natural resources, the ability to influence opinions by controlling information, the extreme centralization of the means to intervene financially, the select-few who have access to weapons of mass destruction, etc.)

'Market' economics and political power of the state, including the military, are today, as they have always been, inseparable. Faced with this unity that has been put in place by capital and transnational oligopolies and the political powers at their service, how then do we build people-centered counter-strategies, which, over and above 'resistance' can actually advance the alternative defined here. This is the real challenge.

Combining the Expansion of Social Movements and the Rebuilding of the Political Citizen

There is no modern society that is stuck in an absolute immutable stage. In this sense, the existence of 'social movements', visible or not, clearly organized or working under wraps, crystallized around a program of objectives defined in political or ideological terms or disregarding for the 'discourses', or 'politician's politics', united or fragmented, is not new.

What is 'new' and characterized by the present movement, is that 'social movements' (or 'civil society') — to use the current fashionable terms — is fragmented, and disregards politics, ideologies, etc. This is, at the same time, the cause but more the product of the erosion of social battle and politics in the prior period of contemporary history (after the second world war), and, because of this, the weakening of their efficiency, and therefore their credibility and legitimacy. This erosion therefore happened within a fundamental disequilibrium, with dominant capital taking advantage of this vacuum, and

3

submitting people and societies to the exclusive logic of its demands, to proclaim the eternity of its 'reign', to pretend that it is rational and even beneficial (the end of history, etc.), that is to say, the permanent utopia of capitalism. This conjuncture manifests itself with absurdities like 'there is no alternative' or in the imagination of a 'social movement' that has the ability to transform the world without defining its targets and plans.

'Social movements'– in plural – exist, and are reinforcing their presence and their actions everywhere throughout the world. It is not even necessary to give examples: classes, and class struggles, democracy movements, women's rights, rights of nations, peasants, environmentalists, are just some of its expressions. The transformation of the world by the crystallization of the alternative can only happen by active involvement in these movements. But it also demands that they know how to progressively go from the defensive to the offensive, from fragmentation to convergence in diversity, in order to become decisive players in inventive and efficient projects to build political strategies aimed at citizens.

Recognizing the weaknesses in the present movement is neither to denigrate it, nor to take a nostalgic glance at a past that is over, but to choose to act to reinforce its emancipatory potential.

The people's adversary is oligarchic and globalized capital and dominant imperialism, the totality of political powers which, for the moment, are totally at its service, that is to say the governments of the triad (since both the right and the left share the same penchant for 'liberalism'), most notably the United States (in which the establishment of Republican and Democratic parties share the same vision of their hegemonic role) and those of the ruling classes throughout the South. This adversary deploys an economic, political, ideological and military strategy that uses all of the institutions set up to service it (OECD, the World Bank, IMF, WTO, NATO, etc.) It has its centers of 'reflection' and its meeting places (Davos in particular, but also Universities with their conventional economic departments). They control the 'fashions' and decide the catch words, the discourses they impose: 'democracy' or 'human rights' (understood as a manipulative term), 'war against poverty', 'the erasing of nations' and parallel promotion of 'communities', the war against 'terrorism', etc. The majority of the 'movements' and the activists that lead them, are up until now, always one step behind, answering belatedly — well, or not so well — to their pieces of the strategy or discourse. We must liberate ourselves from these reflexive and defensive positions, taking away our turn and substituting our discourses, our strategies, our objectives, our language. We have a long way to go.

We will only be able to move in this direction if we are able to systematically analyze the adversary's strategy in its global dimensions and its local and segmented expressions. These strategies are a long way from being a monolithic bloc without fail. They are interspersed with contradictions what we need to analyze, get to know, identify and isolate. We need to propose counter-strategies that can take advantage of these very contradictions.

Faced with this urgent need the 'movement(s)', seems to be still quite weak. Because it has not yet acknowledged the importance of this reflection, and the need to draw the conclusion of the necessity for united action, the movement remains fragmented, defensive, and soft in its discourse and propositions (which its adversary knows and takes advantage of). We must therefore advance to levels that make the crystallization of popular forces counter-strategies possible, in their global vision and interdependence, and in their segmented and local expression. It is only when the principles of the alternative are defined and are consistent, and they take flight in programs and actions rich in diversity and convergence in their impact on society. This is when the 'movement' will become a transforming force in history.

The opponent makes sure that our progress is difficult, not only by physical interventions when necessary (police violence, backward democratic steps, support to renewed 'fascist' currents, wars) but also by soothing propositions so the 'movement' remains 'apolitical', 'soft' and one step behind. The 'movementist' ideology contributes to this, since it rejects precisely, and by principle, what we are proposing: the convergence through diversity of a reconstruction of citizen politics. In these conditions, the movements and the organizational forms that support them (specifically the NGOs, which are now often considered to be the exclusive manifestation of civil society) must be examined critically. Do they adhere to the perspective of the construction of alternatives? Or, are they the system's management technique for its real ambitions — using them as 'anti-alternative' instruments?

Only the rebuilding of citizen politics will allow the 'movement' to acquire the scope that calls into question the disequilibria operating to the favor of capital. Only this rebuilding will allow for the emergence of new social equilibriums and politics that constrain capital to 'adjust' to demands that do not come out of its exclusive logic — forcing people to adapt to the demands of capital as opposed to forcing capital to adapt to the demands of people.

Our call is addressed to everyone — ourselves included — to everyone who finds themselves involved in various actions and meetings around the World Social Forum (Porto Alegre) and in national and regional forums. The World

Forum of Alternatives will act as a catalyst—with and among others—for the elaboration of popular, efficient and credible counter-strategies.

The propositions which follow are just propositions—which some will evaluate as erroneous, extreme or provocative. However, in my opinion, they are worth discussion.

The Collective Imperialism of the Triad, the Hegemonic Offensive of the United States and the Militarization of Globalization

First Thesis

The global system is not 'post imperialist'—it is imperialist. It shares with other previous imperialist systems which always commanded the expansion of global capitalism several fundamental and permanent characteristics: it offers to the people on the periphery (the South, to use the current patois)— three quarters of the population—no chance to 'catch up' and benefit, for better or for worse, the 'advantages' of the level of material consumption reserved for the majority of the people in the centers; it only produces, and reproduces, the deepening of the 'North/South' gap.

Imperialism, nevertheless, has, in many ways, entered into a new phase of its expansion. This has a direct relationship to transformations in capitalism and capital: technological revolution, transformation of the workplace, globalized financial domination, etc. These relationships are the subject of serious research and animated debates. But once again the overall tone is directed by economic obsession of some and the genteel 'soft' politics of others. This happens up to the point where the system is often presented as offering a chance to all those who want to take it. This speaks to the weakness of the 'movement' and the efficiency of the dominant discourse.

I must insist on another new dimension of imperialism. Imperialism, which used to always be referred to in the plural, since permanent and violent, economic and political conflict, between the various imperial centers, were always at the forefront of history, is now referred to in the singular—it has become the collective imperialism of the 'triad' (the United States, Europe, and Japan).

The facts clearly illustrate the reality of the collective character of this new state of imperialism. In all the global economy's managing institutions, Europe and Japan are never singled out for positions that are different than those of the United States, whether it be in the World Bank, the IMF, or the WTO (we remember the demands imposed in Doha in 2001 on the WTO by the European envoy Pascal Lamy on the Third World as being even more severe than those of the United States).

What are the reasons behind this common vision of the triad? Up to what point is the solidarity that they display defining a new stable step in imperialistic globalization? And where can we find the eventual contradictions within the triad?

It has been the custom to explain this solidarity by political reasons: the common concern about the Soviet Union and 'communism'. But the disappearance of this threat did not end this 'Northern' common front, however, Europe and Japan are no longer dependent on the United States, as they were immediately following the Second World War. Having become serious rivals, one could have expected that their conflicts would have destroyed the triad. By agreeing on the same globalized neoliberal project, they, in fact, did exactly the opposite. I am therefore strongly tempted to explain this choice by the new demands of capital accumulation by the dominant oligopolies. They have since forth attained a level of growth that has never before been seen. Their sheer size has forced the oligopolies (the large transnationals that have their anchors in the states of the triad) to need — for their own reproduction — access to a global open market. For some, this new fact means that an authentic transnational capital, and therefore transnational bourgeoisie, is in the making. This question clearly merits more profound research. For others (including myself), that extreme conclusion is not needed, since the common interests in managing the global market place are strong enough to be at the root of transnational capital's solidarity.

The contradictions that could have destroyed the triad, or at least weakened its collective strength, do not lie in the divergent interests of the dominant segments of capital. Their origin should be found elsewhere, since if capital and states are inseparable concepts and realities, the triad — and even its European segment — remain constituted in singular political states. The state cannot be reduced to its functions as a service provider for dominant capital. Articulated by all the contradictions that characterize society — class conflicts, different aspects of the political culture of the people in question, the diversity of national 'collective' interests, and the geo-political expressions of their defense — the state is a distinct player of capital. And what will this complex dynamic bring about? The submission to immediate and exclusive interests of dominant-capital? Or other combinations that regulate the demands of the reproduction of capital and those that manifest themselves in other fields?

In the first hypothesis, with the lack of an integrated common political institution for the states of the triad, the United States, the commander in chief, will be asked to fill the demands of this 'global' state, indispensable for the 'good governance' of globalized capitalism. And the partners in the triad will accept the consequences. However, in this case, I would argue that the 'European project' would be devoid of content, reduced to, — in the best case — the European segment of collective imperialism, or — in the worst case — the European section of the American hegemonic project. For the moment, the ripples that we hear from time to time are due to the political and military management of globalization, not its economic and social management. In other words, certain European powers would prefer a 'collective' political management of the global system, while others accept complete management by the United States.

Whereas in the second hypothesis, that is to say if the European people manage to impose on dominant capital the terms of a new historic compromise which defines the content of European states and the European Union, Europe could hope to be an autonomous player. In other words, the option (and the battles) for a 'Social Europe' (that is to say if power was not simply about being at the immediate and exclusive service of dominant capital) is inseparable from a 'non-American' Europe. And this can only happen if Europe distances itself from the management of collective imperialism by which the interests of dominant-capital defines itself. In one sentence: Europe will be on the 'Left' (with the understanding that this definition means taking into consideration the social interests of European peoples and innovations in North/South relations which will bring about a real post-imperialist evolution) or it won't.

Second Thesis

The hegemonic strategy of the United States is articulated on the collective character of new imperialism and to the profit of the insufficiencies and weaknesses of the 'anti-neoliberal' social and political movements.

This strategy, barely recognized by the 'pro-American' defenders, is, in the dominant discourse, the object of two 'soft' propositions, not quite real, but operational, from the point of view of our opponent. The first is that this hegemony belongs to a 'gentle' leadership, sometimes known as 'benign hegemony' by the democratic fraction of the American establishment. Through this mix of false naivety and real hypocrisy, this discourse pretends that the United States only acts in the interests of the peoples who are associated with the triad, motivated by the same 'democratic' pulses, and even the interests of the rest of the world, to whom globalization offers the chance of 'development', reinforced by the benefits of democracy that American powers promote everywhere, as we know. The second is that, in all domains, the United States benefit from enormous advantages — whether it be economic, scientific, political, military or cultural that legitimize their hegemony. In fact, American hegemony works from logic, and a system, that has little to do with the discourse it envelops.

The objectives of this hegemony have been proclaimed, and adhered to in innumerable productions from the US leaders (unfortunately, little read by its victims). After the fall of the USSR — their only potential military adversary — the US establishment evaluates that it has a period of about 20 years to put into place its global hegemony and reduce to nothingness the possibilities of its potential 'rivals', not that they are necessarily capable of an alternative hegemony, just capable of affirming their autonomy in a global system that would be 'non-hegemonic' — in my language, a multi-centric system. These 'rivals' are of course Europe (we no longer hear talks about a Japan hegemony!), but also Russia and most of all China, the principal designated adversary that Washington may have to envision destroying (militarily) if she continues to persist in her 'development' and a certain independent will. Other rivals have also been noted, in fact, all Southern countries that may develop a resistance to the exigencies of globalized neoliberalism — India or Brazil, Iran or South Africa.

The objectives are therefore to vassalize the allies in the triad, to make them incapable of effective global initiatives, and to destroy the 'large countries', always by nature too 'big' (the United States being the only one with the right to be so). Dismantle Russia after the USSR, dismantle China, India, even Brazil; instrumentalising the weaknesses of each country's power systems, manipulate the former states of the USSR, and stroke the centrifugal forces in the Russian Federation, support the Muslims of Xinjiang and the Tibetan monks, feeding the conflict with the Muslims of the Indian sub-continent, intervening in the Amazon (Plan Colombia), etc.

In this strategic perspective the United States decided that their first strike would be in the region that extends from the Balkans to central Asia, and traverses the Middle East and the Gulf. Why this region for the first American wars of the 21st Century? Not because the region could shelter serious enemies, exactly the opposite, because it is the soft under-belly of the global system, made up of societies, that, for different reasons, right now, are incapable of responding to aggression with even a minimum amount of efficiency. Striking against the weakest to begin a long series of wars — a clear and banal military strategy. Just as Hitler started by attacking Czechoslovakia, while his ambitions went above and beyond this to the United Kingdom, France and Russia.

Conquering the region also presents other opportunities. A major producer of oil and gas, the exclusive control of the United States would make Europe seriously dependent, reducing any eventual maneuverability. Additionally, the installation of American bases at the heart of Eurasia will facilitate the wars of the future, against China, Russia and others. The unconditional support of Israeli expansion is logical within this perspective, Israel being a de facto permanent military base at Washington's service.

The decision to militarize the management of a global system was not taken just by the team of Bush Jr. It has been the rallying call of the ruling classes of the United States since the fall of the USSR; Democrats and Republicans only differ on their choice of language. Moreover, contrary to what they would like naïve opinion holders to believe, this option is meant to mitigate the insufficiencies of the American economy, in which the competitiveness of all the segments of the productive system have continually deteriorated, as witnessed by the trading deficit that characterizes it. By imposing themselves not as the 'natural leader' via its economic advances, but as the military dictator of the world order, the United States is creating conditions that force its vassalized 'allies' (Europe, Japan), similar to others, to pay their deficit. The United States has become a parasitic society that can not maintain its level of consumption and waste without impoverishing the rest of the world.

Third Thesis

The present time is one of extreme gravity. In this sense, comparisons with the 1930s are mostly justifiable. Like Hitler, the President of the United States has decided to replace the law with brutal military force; thereby erasing all the conquests that democracy's victory over Fascism has permitted, condemning the United Nations to the same lamentable fate as the League of Nations.

Alas, the comparisons can continue. Fabrication and choosing minor adversaries to lay the ground work for major confrontations. Systematic lying. The dominant classes of the 'allies' act like Chamberlain and Daladier with Hitler; they cede to, and even sometimes contribute to legitimizing American wars in the eyes of those they are deceiving.

The 'movement' has to understand that faced with this coherent and criminal strategy of its opponent, no counter-strategy can be effective if it does have the battle against American wars as the principal axis of its action.

10

Today, what are the discourses on 'poverty' or 'human rights' worth, when compared to what is in store for people in a far-worse future, which will be imposed by military violence? These wars, still 'small' (despite the gigantic material and human destruction of its victims) — do not constitute 'a problem among other', but the harbinger of the enemy's strategy.

Elements for a Popular Counter-Strategy

The aforementioned reflections — if they make sense — can only lead to one conclusion: the principal axis of actions to come can only be about the organization of actions against 'American wars' and the construction of a large front, composed of all the forces that could be in opposition. In this spirit, I will offer three propositions:

First proposition: A priority in Europe for the reconstruction of a citizen politics, capable of converging the demands of the movements that remain terribly fragmented.

The construction of this political force and the gathering of the subject that could compose it is conditional on the success of the movements in their social and protest demands, that is to say, the ability to renovate a real left faced with European integration which would give a 'social dimension' to the aforementioned project. Equally, it is with this condition that the left could separate from the pro-imperialist right, which accepts the alignment of the United States' imperialist strategies, or if it expresses the wish for 'collective political management' of collective imperialism. In other words, there will never be a 'Social Europe' if there is no simultaneous engagement toward 'another politics' vis-à-vis the rest of the world, which would take up a real post-imperialist transition.

European people can and must make the United States aware of the fragility of their position in the economic system of globalized capitalism. If they manage to impose the use of their capital surpluses for social development, instead of its current role of supporting American waste, they will simultaneously constrain the United States and force them to abandon their excessive ambitions. This strategic objective clearly does not exclude the immediate support of the courageous men and women who, at the heart of the system, are saying 'No to war'. Nevertheless, I remain skeptical about the effectiveness of the internal opposition in the United States, as long as the privileges of this parasitic society will remain guaranteed. The American ruling class has managed to obtain a dominant public opinion sufficiently foolish, that the protests of the conscious minority are not able to bring down the deployment of the United States' hegemonic strategy.

Second proposition: Encourage a rapprochement between the large Euro-Asian partners — namely, Europe, Russia, China, and India.

Russia, with its oil and gas reserves, offers Europe its only means to escape the American diktat, assuming that Washington is successful in its plans to have exclusive control over the Middle East. And since a majority of the foreign trade and investment Russia attracts is from Europe and not the United States, there is already favorable ground for a rapprochement between Europe and Russia, in spite of the difficulties (produced by the 'comprador' management of the Russian economy in which important fractions of the new ruling class are associated with) and the manipulation of American imperialism, which brings its support to the centrifugal forces operating in Russia and other former states of the USSR. Here again, as in Europe, a favorable evolution benefiting the working class implies another foreign policy, which distances itself from Washington.

The rapprochement of Russia, China and India would find its raison-d'être in the — military — threat that these three countries will face with the eventual success of the United States' deployments in Central Asia. American diplomacy is making this rapprochement as difficult as possible by mobilizing, to its benefit, the contradictions of the political visions of each of the three partners and in supporting the compradors fractions of the ruling classes. But, over and above the geo-political conflicts that make up the border questions between China and India, or Tibet and the Xinjiang, over and above Washington's manipulations that 'support' India against China and at the same time agitate Pakistan and provoke conflicts between India's Muslims and Hindus, the strategy of the popular forces — defined at this stage by the demands of the constitution of an anti-compradors front — has to take in once again, here and elsewhere, the measure of the direct relations that comprador management (in place in Russia and India, and threatening in China) maintains with the demands of American geo-political diktats.

Third proposition: Revive Afro-Asian peoples solidarity (the spirit of Bandung), bring back to life the 'Tricontinental'.

This solidarity between people of the South runs today through their struggle against comprador powers that is produced and supported by 'liberal' globalization. The themes elaborated above concerning the alternative — social progress, democratization, national autonomy — will find here their raison d'être.

There is little doubt that the legitimacy of these compradors powers is being questioned in many countries of the South. Nevertheless, the responses of the people of the South to the challenges they face from the new imperial system and liberalization make it difficult to advance alternatives that are defined in terms of democratization, social progress and the construction of a just and negotiated global inter-dependence. For different reasons, including the erosion of national populism formulas which were characteristic of the preceding period and that emerged from national liberation movements and autocratic practices of political management (despite the 'democratic' rhetoric), still dominate in a number of countries, the disarrayed popular classes frequently find refuge in illusions that are 'fundamentalist', ethnic or religious, which are mostly manipulated by the local comprador ruling classes, which are supported by imperialism and particularly by the US. These consist of real step backs, which need lucidity and courage to fight; and today, they constitute a major obstacle to the rebuilding of solidarity between the Afro-Asian peoples (by intensifying the often criminal conflicts between Muslim and Hindus here, Hutu and Tutsi over there, etc.). The impasse that constitutes these communal regressions finds its extreme manifestation in questionable characters like the Taliban, Bin Laden, or Sadam Hussein, who were themselves the beneficiaries of the generous support of the CIA, only to become the United States' 'Public Enemy number one' and could, by this fact, appear like that in the eyes of large swaths of popular opinion.

The counter-point is being drawn here from the reconstruction of national, popular and democratic alliances, like those that brought down some dictators (Mali being a prime example), but also apartheid in South Africa, and that also brought about Lula's victory in Brazil. These advances — modest when we consider the present dominance of imperialist aggression — are nevertheless potential harbingers of the renaissance of the Southern Peoples Front.

In conclusion: the struggle for social justice, democracy, and a multi-centric equal international order are inseparable. The United States establishment understands it perfectly. This is why they are moving ahead to implement their own hegemonic international order, by substituting the use of brutal military force to international law and justice. And knowing that — for them — is the only means to impose an unequal neoliberal social order, condemning democracy, where it exists, to degradation, and making it impossible elsewhere. Resistance movements and people's struggles must understand

13

this. They must understand that their plans for social and democratic progress have no future, if the United States' plan for military hegemony is not stopped.

2

An African Perspective on Nine Eleven

Mahmood Mamdani

This talk is about a single event, September 11, 2001. How should we think of 9/11? What led to it? What are its likely consequences? One explanation is already on offer. It is an explanation I call Culture Talk.

We now speak of the period after the Cold War as the era of globalization. Culture Talk is the language of contemporary globalization. The newly globalized world is culture-coded. Culture has replaced society as a key organizing concept for classifying and ordering social reality. From this point of view, global cultural identities are considered more reliable indicators of the state of the world than internal social processes. This new understanding of culture is highly political. It is different from culture as anthropologists understand it: culture as face-to-face, intimate, and local. In contrast, the strategic talk of culture is flattened. It comes in large geo-political packages.

Culture Talk makes two assumptions. The first is that every culture has an essence that defines it. From this point of view, politics is said to be a consequence of culture. Thus, if democracy is Western, then terrorism is said to be Islamic or Arab. The formulation Islamic terrorism is thus offered as both a description and an explanation of the events of 9/11.

The strategic talk of culture also assumes that the world is divided into two: pre-modern and modern. Moderns are said to make culture, and thus to be masters of culture. In contrast, pre-modern culture is said to be more like a twitch, a habit. Rather than make culture, pre-moderns are said to carry their traditions, somewhat in the manner of passengers who carry baggage on a journey: they are not masters, but agents, of culture. Even if pre-moderns can't be held responsible for their actions, it is said that they must be restrained, collectively, if necessary, even held in detention, for the good of civilization.

Before 9/11, Africans were considered the primary example of people resistant to modernity. After 9/11, Muslims and Arabs have taken first place.

The difference is this: Africans were said to be a threat to themselves, and not to anyone else. The Western media termed African violence 'black-on-black' violence. Muslims are said to be worse, a threat to themselves and to others.

Here, I shall present an alternative explanation to Culture Talk, an explanation more political and historical. 9/11 was not born of a deep-seated clash of civilizations but of a more recent history. To make sense of it, I will put 9/11 in the context of the Cold War. My perspective on the Cold War will be from an African location. My explanation will link both types of violence said to be cultural, 'black-on-black' violence and 'Islamic terrorism,' and locate them in a single dynamic, the Late Cold War.

Some Observations on Fundamentalism

I want to begin with some observations on fundamentalism. Fundamentalism is a term invented in 1920 by a Protestant clergyman in the United States, Rev. Curtis Lee Laws. Rev. Curtis Lee Laws belonged to the Presbyterians of Princeton who defended the fundamentals of Christianity against Church liberals. Specifically, they defended five fundamental truths from the Scriptures as literal and infallible: fundamentals such as the virgin birth of Christ, the resurrection of Christ, the objective reality of miracles, and so on. Between 1910 and 1915, they issued 13 paperback pamphlets, each in three million copies. Called The Fundamentals, these were sent to every pastor, professor and theology student in the country.

Fundamentalism was born as a struggle inside religion, not between religions; it was a struggle inside civilization, not between civilizations. In 1925, the legislature of the state of Tennessee criminalized the teaching of evolution. A few months later, Scopes, a biology teacher in a Tennessee school confessed that he had taught Darwin's theory of evolution in a biology class. The Scopes Trial took place in 1925. It pitted a well-known Democratic politician and former Presidential candidate, William Jennings Bryant, against an equally well-known lawyer representing the liberal American Civil Liberties Union. The elderly Bryant was humiliated in court: he had to admit that a literal definition of the Bible was not defensible, that the world could not have been created in six days, and that it was not only 5,000 years old. Made a fool of in court, he died two days later.

Protestant Fundamentalists exiled themselves from American public life after the trial. They created their own institutions. This fundamentalist counter-culture was typified by Bob Jones University, created in 1927.

The fundamentalists returned to political life in the US in two phases: the first after World War 2 in the 1950s, and the second after the Civil Rights movement in the 1970s. The first wave was led by the Evangelicals. They argued against fundamentalist separation and exile, and for uniting with other conservative Christians. They were led by 'televangelists,' particularly Billy Graham, who rapidly became the favourite spiritual counselor for most American Presidents.

The second wave of fundamentalist return followed the 1973 decision of the US Supreme Court, Roe vs. Wade, that abortion is a woman's natural right. It also led fundamentalists to direct involvement in politics. Jerry Fallwell challenged the Christian right to learn from Black Churches and the Civil Rights Movement. Fallwell formed the Moral majority in 1979, and called on Christians to change history. He said that the idea that 'politics and religion should not mix' is an idea of the devil meant to keep Christians from running their own country!

Fallwell gave political sermons, called Jeremiads. He defined abortion as a biological Holocaust, and AIDS as a judgment of God against immorality, abortion and homosexuality. The major achievement of Protestant Fundamentalism was to stop the passage of the Equal Rights Amendment, the constitutional amendment that was to grant equal rights to men and women in the United States.

By the mid-1970s, Gallup Polls showed that a third of adult Americans, roughly 50 million, defined themselves as 'born again'. In 1980, fundamentalists organized a 'Washington for Jesus' mass rally in the capital. In 1983, Ronald Reagan, a 'born-again' President, addressed the National Association of Evangelicals, and called the Soviet Union 'an evil empire'.

At the 1992 Republican Convention in Houston, Texas, the Christian Right candidate Patrick Buchanan warned of a coming 'religious war'. I quote him: 'It is a cultural war, as critical to the kind of nation we shall be, as the Cold War itself, for this war is for the soul of America'. When 9/11 happened, Jerry Fallwell and Pat Robertson publicly proclaimed it 'a judgment of God for the sins of the secular humanists in the United States'.

Later, I shall have something to say about two related issues: the involvement of the religious right in US foreign policy during the Reagan Administration, and the growing link between Christian Right and the Jewish Zionist Right after 9/11.

For now, I want to sum up this brief historical overview by emphasizing an important historical difference between Islam and Christianity. Unlike Christianity, mainstream Islam has no institutional religious hierarchy parallel to the secular hierarchy of the state. What we call

Christian Fundamentalism describes the entry of Christian clergy into secular politics. Contemporary Islamist politics shows us a reverse movement: the movement of secular intellectuals into the religious domain. This is why I think it is more accurate to speak of political Islam than of Islamic fundamentalism. If Protestant fundamentalism developed at the initiative of the clergy, political Islam is more of an initiative of political intellectuals. The key figures in the development of political Islam in the 20th century are Mawdudi, and Indian, and later Pakistani, journalist, Sayyed Qutb, an Egyptian literary and educational scholar, and Ali Shariati, an Iranian humanist intellectual. These are intellectuals, not religious leaders. The major exception to this generalization is Ayatollah Khomeini in Iran. Faced with Ali Shariati, the political intellectual, Khomeini turned the *ulema*, Islamic jurists, into constitutional custodians of sovereignty, in the constitutional arrangement he called Vilayat al Fiqh.

My basic point is that the development of a fundamentalist trend in Christianity has no parallel in either Islam or other religions. In Islam, as in Hinduism, extremist religious politics has been the work of political intellectuals to which the clergy has been forced to respond.

Contemporary political Islamist thought is differentiated between two major tendencies, the societal and the state-oriented, with contradictory political implications. The project of the societal tendency has been to create Islamist social movements for social reform. In contrast, the state-oriented tendency has lacked confidence in popular organization and action and so has been suspicious of any societal project. Statist intellectuals have either been incorporated in existing Islamist regimes, such as in Pakistan or Saudi Arabia, or they have functioned as isolated groups in opposition to existing states and at a distance from social movements.

My argument will be that political terror is the work of statist tendencies, not social movements. The real question we need to face today, in the aftermath of 9/11, is: how did this strain, otherwise typified by isolated and highly factionalized small groups, take the leap from the word to the deed, from thought to action? It required a multiplication of numbers and, beyond it, their organization, training, and resourcing, so as to increase their reach and, ultimately, their confidence.

The answer to this question should underline an important lesson: Terrorism is not a religious tendency. It is a political tendency, born of a political encounter, during the Late Cold War. That encounter will be the subject of this talk.

The Late Cold War

I was a young lecturer at the University of Dar-es-Salaam in 1975. The year 1975 was a momentous one: it was the year the US was defeated in Vietnam and the year the last European empire in Africa collapsed. Together, these two events made for a shift in the centre of gravity of the Cold War, from southeast Asia to southern Africa. After the collapse of the Portuguese empire in Africa, who would pick up the pieces: the US or the Soviet Union?

I refer to the period after 1975 as the Late Cold War. The shift of US strategy during the Late Cold War was defined by two lessons from the war in Indochina. One was drawn by the Executive and was called the Nixon Doctrine. The other was drawn by the legislature in the form of the Clark Amendment.

The two lessons came from two different but related wars, one in Vietnam, the other in Laos. The Vietnam War involved hundreds of thousands of US troops on the ground; it was 'Americanized'. In contrast, a 1962 Treaty between Moscow and Washington prevented the entry of US ground troops into Laos. To circumvent this limitation, the US improvised a two-fold strategy in Laos: war by proxy, supported by a ferocious air war. War by proxy involved the organization of a private, ethnically-organized army of 30,000 Hmong fighters. This mercenary army was directed by a Hmong warlord, Gen. Vang Pao, and was funded by an extremely lucrative and rapidly growing trade in opium.

A young Yale PhD. student travelled to Vietnam and Laos in the 1970s to research the political economy of opium production, and its processing into high-grade opium for the fast growing numbers of US soldiers in Vietnam. Let me sum up, in a nut shell, the findings he elaborated in his PhD. thesis. Opium was grown in Hmong villages; the US aid establishment financed the construction of 150 landing strips to make these villages accessible by air. A CIA plane, called Air America, collected the opium from scattered villages and took it to a heroin processing laboratory owned by Gen. Vang Pao, situated right next to the CIA headquarters in Laos. The irony, of course, is that the CIA provided political cover for a trade in opium and heroin that got roughly 15 per cent of US troops addicted to heroin to some degree, according to studies done by the US army itself.

The proxy war on the ground was backed up by a wholly American war from the air. It is in Laos that the US discovered a new war doctrine: unlike previous assumptions, the air force can win a war, provided there are no political limits on the intensity of its bombing, and therefore the extent of destruction of civilian life and property. Official America would later describe the destruction of civilian lives and livelihood by a single arid term, 'collateral damage'.

The Laos bombing was unprecedented in intensity, even by the standards of Second World War. A group of Cornell university scientists concluded that the bombing had violated the principle of proportionality between gain sought and the damage caused, a principle governments at war were required to observe by the Geneva Convention on War. Neil Sheehan, the Pulitzer Prize-winning *New York Times* journalist wrote: 'The air war may constitute a war crime by the American government and its leaders'.

The closing years of the war in Indochina coincided with a surge of anti-war sentiment in the US. As a result, a number of anti-war Congressmen and women were elected to the legislature, Senate and House. Their influence led to the passage of a number of anti-war legislations, such as the War Powers Act, the Freedom of Information Act and the Clark Amendment which prohibited the Executive, including the Pentagon and the CIA, from providing any kind of aid to combatants in the Angolan civil war.

While the Clark Amendment lasted, which was for a decade, from 1975 to 1985, the Executive looked for ways to sidestep legislative accountability. In that context, the lessons of Laos became relevant. Of immediate significance was the precedent of a proxy war, a war fought through second and third parties, and therefore with no accountability to US Congress. In contrast, the Laotian precedent of a ferocious air war with no political limits on the destruction of civilian life and livelihood could only be revived after the collapse of the Soviet Union and the emergence of unrivalled American global supremacy. The first use of unlimited American air power after Laos was in the Gulf War in 1991.

The point I wish to pursue here is this. After defeat in Vietnam and the Watergate Scandal at home, and faced with strong anti-war sentiment at home, official America decided to harness, even cultivate, terrorism against regimes that it considered pro-Soviet and, therefore, fair game. This lesson was first developed in southern Africa, and later in central America and central Asia. These three global locations mark three successive phases in the Late Cold War. Each phase was the source of a new lesson. Together, they can be plotted as a single learning curve.

Southern Africa

As the decolonization movement gathered momentum in Portugal's African colonies in the mid-seventies, official America looked to apartheid South Africa as its much-needed regional ally. The partnership between official America and apartheid South Africa bolstered two key movements that practised a varying mixture of terrorism and politics at different points of its existence: Renamo in Mozambique, and Unita in Angola (Minter 1994:2-5, 142-49, 152-68; Vines 1991:24, 39; Brittain 1988:63). This similarity should in no way blur important differences between Renamo and Unita. Renamo began as no more than a counter-insurgency operation, one that was compelled to learn the art of political organization as a survival strategy, whereas Unita began as a political movement that learnt the practice of counter-insurgency along the way. Renamo was a quintessentially terrorist movement that targeted civilians; in contrast, Unita was more of a political movement whose resort to terror was from tactical rather than strategic considerations.

Renamo was created by the Rhodesian army in the 1970s. After the end of white rule in Rhodesia in 1980, it was patronized by the South African army. The US never supported Renamo directly. Yet, it warmly supported South Africa in just that period when the South African army moved to control levers of government, and to shift regional policy from détente to 'total onslaught'. The Reagan Administration rationalized its embrace of apartheid South Africa as 'constructive engagement,' a move that directly undercut internal South African pressures for reform of apartheid after the 1976 Soweto uprising. Over time, Renamo combined direct South African support with a policy that took advantage of unpopular Frelimo policies, such as forced labour and forced villagization.

How can we define official American responsibility in the spread of political terror in Mozambique? The US did not directly support terror, not in Mozambique; specific branches of the US government, like the State Department, even documented and denounced the destruction of civilian life and livelihood by Renamo. At the same time, 'constructive engagement' provided a political cover for all those involved in the pursuit of terror for political purposes. Without official America looking the other way, apartheid South Africa could not have pursued a policy of terror in Mozambique and Angola with impunity.

Africa had no prior experience of a war that unleashed political terror deliberately on civilians. Renamo was the first example of a combat whose targets were not military, but civilian. This was the opposite of guerrilla struggle. Whereas guerrillas who saw themselves as fish in water, the point of terror was to drain the water and isolate the fish. Terrorists distinguished between victims and targets. Even if water got drained and all other forms of life were destroyed, this was an unintended consequence, simply collateral damage.

21

I don't want to give the impression that there was only one route to the development of political terrorism during the Late Cold War. There were several routes. The imperial search for ways to erode popular support for militant nationalist movements like Frelimo and MPLA was just one. At the same time, I consider this particular route, which led to the development of terrorist movements like Renamo in Mozambique and the Contras in Nicaragua, to be the main route. This is for one reason. Without the strategic embrace of terror by a superpower, there would not have been a global environment of political immunity in which political terror came to flourish.

Let me briefly describe two other routes to the development of political terrorism. A second route was the mirror opposite of the main route pioneered by the US and its proxies. It was the consequence of the internal degeneration of guerrilla movements. The development of vigilante groups and street gangs in the anti-apartheid struggle in South Africa has been amply described in the report of the Truth and Reconciliation Commission. Recent reports testify to similar tendencies inside the PLO and other Palestinian movements. Within our own region, there is the example of SPLA, which has allegedly resorted to forced recruitment through the abduction of youth, even children.

A different route testifies to the development of political terrorism from non-ideological groups, reflecting a profound socio-political crisis without a remedy in sight. The non-ideological route is illustrated by the history and practice of movements like the RUF in Sierra Leone and the LRA in northern Uganda. Both feed off the local population and terrorize it, without making any significant attempt to organize it. At the same time, available research seems to indicate that these movements have drawn their first cadres from the most alienated and marginal sections of the population, precisely those who had been victims of practices of state terrorism.

Let us take a recent example. One day in 1990, armed forces marched into Freetown and raped, pillaged and killed — over 5,000 civilians. The US and British response to the practice of terror, whether by government soldiers or by RUF recruits, was customarily to call for reconciliation. Reconciliation in these contexts was a code word for sharing power with terrorists!

Nicaragua

The Nicaraguan Revolution swept a brutal dictator from power in 1979. Ronald Reagan came to power in the US the following year, in 1980. In November of 1981, President Reagan passed National Security Decision Directive No. 17, authorizing $19.7 million for the CIA to create a paramilitary force for attacks on Nicaragua. Over the years, the CIA developed this paramilitary force, the counter-revolutionaries, called the contras. Two aspects of the relationship between the contras and official America are important for our purposes.

Whereas official America had hitherto only provided a political cover to terrorism, it now got directly engaged in the very development of terrorist movements. Instead of a shy and permissive relationship as in southern Africa, central America gives us an example of an active and brazen cultivation of terror by a superpower. Official America created and supported the contras just as South African/Rhodesian securities had created and supported Renamo.

The Contras used the same tactics as did Renamo: blowing up bridges and health centres, killing health personnel and judges, even heads of cooperatives. A Washington-based human rights group used the Freedom of Information Act to access a CIA manual for contras, called Psychological Operations in Guerrilla Warfare. Mimicking the language of guerrilla warfare, whereby it baptized terrorists as 'guerrillas,' the book called for 'armed propaganda' and advised 'selective use of violence'. Here is how the CIA advocated the selective use of terror: 'If the government police cannot put an end to guerrilla activities, the population will lose confidence in the government which has the inherent mission of guaranteeing the safety of citizens. However, the guerrillas should be careful not to become an explicit terror, because this would result in a loss of popular support'.

The point of terrorism was not to take power or to win civilian support. Its point was to get the government to respond excessively. Its point was perverse: to invite repression so as to discredit the government in the eyes of the citizenry. For the US, the point was also to do this while at the same time denying responsibility for it. Remember that the Contra violence was always explained away as 'Nicaraguans fighting Nicaraguans,' just as the violence in Mozambique, or for that matter in Kwazulu Natal in South Africa, was also explained away as 'Black-on-Black' violence. The claim was that this is just what natives are like, by nature; they simply do not know how to settle differences peacefully, how to live by the rule of law.

Nicaragua also illustrates direct CIA involvement in large-scale terrorist attacks by using regional proxies and individual CIA assets. The best known example was the mining of Nicaraguan harbours. When this created a public furore, US Congress passed the Boland Amendment, which sharply limited official American assistance to the Contras to a quarter of what the Reagan Administration had asked for. The Executive response was to turn to private sources, including drug lords and syndicates, right-wing mercenaries and the religious right. The result was increasingly to privatize the war.

23

The alliance between the CIA and drug lords was one of mutual convenience: the CIA provided political protection, and the drug lords purchased it with illicit funds. Following the Iran-Contra Scandal, the Kerry Committee of the US Senate probed this connection, and provided plenty of examples of the same planes that carried arms for Contras from the US bringing back drugs into the US on the return journey. *The San Jose Mercury*, a major California newspaper, ran a series of reports on how the CIA-connection was critical to the rise of the Medallin Cartel, allowing the Cartel to use Contra connections to bring in cocaine into Los Angeles for sale to black street gangs. The CIA vehemently denied these reports while the Contras were active, only for the CIA internal investigation to confirm these accusations — though only after the Contra war was over and the Sandinistas were out of power.

Oliver North, a member of President Reagan's National Security Council, took the lead in privatizing the war. He was the key link in developing connections, not only with the drug lords, but also with right-wing mercenaries and the Religious Right. The ranks of the latter included Rev. Pat Robertson and Rev. Moon of the Unification Church.

In its support of the Contras, the US also pioneered re-combining terror with politics. It turned to electoral politics to convince the population that the only way to end terror was to hand over power to terrorists. The Sandinistas lost power for two reasons, only one of which points to their own mistakes, whereas the other points to the political windfall of terrorism. This same lesson can be drawn from Charles Taylor coming to power in Liberia.

Afghanistan

Two popular revolutions removed two brutal dictatorships in 1979. One was the Somoza dictatorship in Nicaragua; the other was that of the Shah of Iran. In February of 1979, there took place the first occupation of the US embassy in Iran. Asked by Khomeini and his Prime Minister, Bazargan, to leave, the students brought the occupation to a close. In March, the US welcomed the Shah to New York for medical reasons. A second student occupation followed; this time there was no pressure from the revolutionary government to end it. The students released women and black soldiers; 52 American diplomats were held for 444 days. In September 1980, Sadam Hussein invaded Iran, with enthusiastic US support. The subsequent war saw the first use of chemical weapons after the Vietnam War.

The Afghan War also began in the year 1979. The war was different in several respects. Unlike the Contra war, it was waged on the Soviet border.

24

It was the largest war of the time; the CIA funding for the Afghan War exceeded CIA funding for all covert wars, just as Afghanistan saw the largest foreign mobilization of Soviet troops since the Second World War.

Unlike other proxy wars of regional significance, the US fought the Afghan War through a global alliance. It also fought the Afghan War not for a regional or a national goal — the independence of Afghanistan — but for a strategic global goal: to bleed the Soviet Union white. This single strategic objective shaped the uncompromising tactics of the war, why it was fought as a highly ideological war, and why neither cost nor proportionality seemed to matter. More important for the future of Afghanistan, the US had little interest in either nationalist or moderate or even secular Afghan movements. In this, it was in agreement with Pakistan, which feared Afghani nationalists lest they advocate the unity of Pathan people, currently living on both sides of the Pakistan-Afghan border.

Having decided on the terms of the war as a religious war, as a crusade against the 'evil empire' and a jihad against 'godless communism,' the US took the lead in organizing a global Islamic alliance. It recruited Muslim cadres for the war, from both Muslim-majority countries from Indonesia to Algeria and Pakistan to Sudan, to Muslim minorities from China to Europe and USA. Having embraced a war in which there could be no compromise, only defeat or victory, the Reagan Administration was determined to up the ante, no matter the cost.

On March 1985, President Reagan signed National Security Directive 166, authorizing stepped-up military assistance to the mujahiddin, which is how the anti-Soviet guerrillas were called. With the objective defined as no less than a Soviet defeat, William Casey, the head of the CIA, took three decisions in 1986. The first was to provide American advisors and Stinger missiles to the Afghan guerrillas. The second was to carry the war into the Soviet Republics of Tajikistan and Uzbekistan, and the third was to recruit Muslims from around the world for this Holy War.

The combined effect was to ideologize the war as a religious war of Islam, as a jihad. The history of jihad after the early period of state formation in Islam records only two instances of jihad as a holy war. The first is the war against the Crusaders, led by the Kurdish warrior Saladin, in the 12th century. The second is the war against the Ottoman occupation in Saudi Arabia in the 18th century. Between the Wahhabi jihad in Saudi Arabia and the Late Cold War, there had been no jihad for two centuries. After the Wahhabi jihad, the Saudi monarchy turned the jihad into a state institution against any opposition, internal or external, by championing the notion of a standing jihad as a military institution. It is this Saudi state notion that was taken over by Casey's boys.

25

I have already pointed out that before 1985, the religious right in Islam was divided into two tendencies. Those in power were integrated into pro-American regimes, as in Saudi Arabia and Pakistan. Those opposed to ruling regimes as sell-outs to the cause of Palestine or Islam existed as small groups. They had no program outside of isolated acts of terror.

Let me return to the question I posed at the beginning of this talk. Before the Afghan War, right-wing Islamism was an intellectual ideological tendency with little organization and muscle on the ground. The Afghan War gave it numbers, organization, skills, reach, confidence and a coherent objective. The infrastructure of liberation that America created during the Afghan War in fact turned out to be an infrastructure of terror. How did this happen?

The blueprint for the Afghan jihad was masterminded by the CIA in collaboration with the intelligence services of Pakistan, Saudi Arabia and Egypt, with peripheral involvement from other intelligence organizations, including China, Britain, and even Israel. The CIA procured the funding, the equipment, and military advisors and it did the training of Afghan and Arab trainers outside Pakistan and Afghanistan. Its main partner, Pakistan's Inter-Services Intelligence (ISI), organized internal transport, directly liaised with jihadi organizations and the training of guerrillas inside Pakistan and Afghanistan.

Recruitment was done mainly from Egypt, Saudi Arabia, Sudan, Algeria and other Arab and Islamic countries. The Arab recruits came to be known as the Arab-Afghans. They comprised all kinds of persons, from political dissidents of Islamic persuasion to ardent religious believers, and from adventurers to criminals and psychopaths. There is no consensus on how many Arab-Afghans were trained during the decade of the Afghan War; the estimates range from between 35,000 and 100,000.

The leadership of the Arab Afghans was picked by the Saudi intelligence and approved by the CIA. The key leader was Osama bin Laden. He came from a wealthy and cultured family with close ties to America and the Republican establishment. The Bin Laden family are counted among important donors to charities in the US, and to important educational institutions like Harvard and Yale.

Recruitment of cadres for the war was done mainly through Islamic charities. There is little public information on this. The information I have seen is about recruitment done in North Africa, particularly Tunisia, by the religious charity called Tablighi Jamaat.

To conduct the training of recruits, traditional religious schools, called madrassahs, were militarized. The USAID funded an educational program of $50 million. The entire sum was provided to the University of Nebraska.

Part of the program was the production of children's text-books. Let me give you two examples from two primary school books that were part of American aid to Afghan refugees. You can decide for yourself whether these promoted a civic or a militarized education.

A math book for 9 year olds in 3rd grade asked the following question: 'One group of mujahiddin attack 50 Russian soldiers. 20 Russians are killed. How many Russians fled?' Here is another question, this time from a math book for primary four: 'The speed of a Kalashinkov bullet is 800 meters per second. If a Russian is at a distance of 3200 meters from a mujahiddin, and that mujahiddin aims at the Russian's head, how many seconds will it take for the bullet to strike the Russian in the forehead?'

With private recruitment and private training, there was a trend to privatizing the Afghan War. At the same time, the more the Afghan War got privatized, the more it led to the privatization of knowledge on how to manufacture and produce violence. The 1993 bombing of the World Trade Center Towers was a strong warning. The proceedings at the court trial in New York revealed that the suspects were CIA-trained in the Afghan War; the bomb they used had been made according to chemical processes prescribed in a CIA handbook.

When it came to financing the war, the CIA followed the lessons it had learnt since the Second World War, from the port city of Marseilles to Burma, and Laos to Central America. Not surprisingly, with the Afghan War too, the drug trade turned out to be a major source of funds. The key beneficiary of CIA funds was Gulbuddin Hikmatyar. Famed as the most radical of the political Islamists, Hikmatyar was also Afghanistan's major drug lord. He alone controlled seven heroin refineries across the border in Pakistan.

When the US first announced that it would materially support resistance to the Soviet Union in Afghanistan, Dr. Musto, a Yale University professor who was also a medical member of the White House Drug Council, resigned. He later told Alfred McCoy, the Yale University researcher I cited earlier, 'I told the [White House Drug] Council that we were going into Afghanistan to support the opium growers in their battle against the Soviets. Shouldn't we try to avoid what we had done in Laos?'

Here are some other findings from Alfred McCoy's research on the connections of the Afghan War with the opium and heroin trade. Whenever the mujahiddin came to control an area, they imposed the growing of heroin as a 'revolutionary tax' on peasants. The opium was collected by opium lords in Afghanistan and sold to heroin lords who controlled the processing laboratories across the border in Pakistan. The opium and the heroin lords were among the most important leaders of the Afghan anti-Soviet struggle. In an arrangement that resembled that between the Contras and the Medallin

27

Cartel in Central America, the Pakistani army provided transport from the border in the same sealed convoys that brought weapons to the border. The CIA provided legal cover: from roughly the time the CIA began organizing the Contras in Nicaragua, a Presidential directive affirmed that no CIA 'asset' could be convicted on drug charges. The directive was only repealed after the Afghan War, quietly, under the Clinton Administration. We can gauge the significance of the opium trade from figures provided by the UN Drug Control Program. Insignificant when the anti-Soviet War began in 1979, opium production in Afghanistan reached a whopping 71 per cent of global production in 1990, the year after the war ended.

Gulbudding Hikmatyar's group received more than half of all CIA-provided arms in the course of the Afghan War. Three million Afghan refugees flowed into Pakistan in the course of the war. With his control over weapons provided by the CIA and provisions from the US government and American NGOs, Hikmatyar controlled the bulk of supplies to refugee camps. He used this both to control the camps and to fight rival mujahiddin organizations.

The largest battle in the Afghan jihad took place in 1988–89. It did not pit the mujahiddin against the Soviet army or the Afghan government; it pit two mujahiddin drug lords against each other. On one side was Mulla Nasim who controlled the largest opium fields in the valley; on the other was Gulbuddin Hikmatyar who controlled the heroin labs across the border in Pakistan.

When the Soviets left, rival mujahiddin factions, including drug lords, fought one another for control over the capital city, Kabul. The fight for Kabul was more fierce than any battle the mujahiddin had fought against the Soviets. In this battle, different factions bombed different sections of their own city.

With rival mujahiddin factions raping women and looting civilians at road blocks, it is not surprising that when the students in the madrassahs organized as the Taliban — remember that the word Talib means students, and Taliban is its plural form — the population eagerly supported the Taliban who championed law and order. But the law was patriarchal. It codified unequal treatment, even violent treatment, against women and youth.

The Afghan War had been fought by two groups: local Afghan recruits and Arab-Afghans recruited internationally by the CIA. When the war ended, the Afghan recruits could go home. But the Arab-Afghans had no home to return to. When a few did return, they were imprisoned by Arab governments, aware that the returnees were trained in lethal methods and organized in numbers. The result was that most stayed on in Afghanistan. As the US walked away, its purpose served, it left yesterday's liberation fighters

28

literally stranded, without home, country, even family. In their hour of need, they were provided protection and purpose by a leadership around Osama bin Laden, which set up an organization called The Base — *al Qaeda* in Arabic. It provided welfare and training for Arab-Afghans, and it pledged to continue waging the jihad, to take the fight to the lone superpower. I shall return to this question later. For now, it is sufficient to note that this was not the first time in history that yesterday's allies had fallen out. In American street slang, the chickens had come home to roost.

The United States: A Democratic Empire

I want to close with a word on the lone superpower and the challenge we face today, how to defend freedom in the face of such overwhelming power. Let me begin by underlining a peculiarity that distinguishes modern Western empires from empires in history. Historically, empires have made little distinction between nationals and non-nationals: all have been held by the emperor and his court in different degrees of subjugation. The distinctiveness of Western empires flows from nationalism, a product of the modern West. Western empires distinguish between citizens and subjects. The former are nationals, the latter are part of the empire. That distinction is being drawn more sharply in America today than it was before 9/11.

The US is a democratic empire. Internally, relations between rulers and ruled are regulated through a set of freedoms, including the freedom of information and organization. American citizens are substantially free to organize in opposition to official American policies, including foreign policy. The lesson of Vietnam is the importance of internal opposition to the war. It is the anti-war movement that circumscribed the full unleashing of US power.

After the Vietnam War, the executive held the press responsible for losing the war. It responded with a concerted attempt to control the press. This was possible for several reasons. One, soon after Vietnam came 'the killing fields' of Cambodia. The American Presidency held the Press responsible for the massacres, for reporting only 'our atrocities,' never 'their atrocities'. Since then, the tendency in the press has been to report the American government version of 'their atrocities'. Just compare how the American press reported the Gulf War with reportage on Vietnam. Second, media ownership also changed hands. Key television channels were bought over by interests located in either the defence or the entertainment industry. Third, there is the question of Israel. There is significant press censorship when it comes to Israel. This is not just true of the Jewish-owned press, like the *New York Times*. It is also true of the non-Jewish press, like the *Boston Globe*. Why?

Why the exaggerated significance of Israel in American society? There have been many answers to this question. They range from the power of the Israeli lobby to the lure of oil to Israel's strategic importance for the US All of these highlight special interests with a pro-Israeli bias. None explain why Israel evokes a mainstream resonance, among both men and women, and across the range of America's multi-cultural society.

To understand this, we need to appreciate what is historically specific about the American experience. Africa and America are names for two radically different political experiences. With the end of apartheid, Africa stands for the defeat of settler colonialism. America, in contrast, stands for the triumph of settler colonialism. The American tendency, both official and unofficial, is to see the world through settler-colonial lenses. To an average American, there is nothing abnormal about settler-colonialism.

I believe American responses to major catastrophes in their history confirms this observation. After the end of slavery, Americans found a solution in the return of slaves to their native land, Africa, even if these natives would return after an absence of centuries and generations. Remember, Liberia was established as a home for returning former slaves from America, and Sierra Leone for those returning from Britain, really those American slaves who had fought with the British Army against American settlers.

The second major catastrophe in American history was the Holocaust. America took the lead in establishing Israel, just as it had earlier established Liberia. Israel was to be a home for returning natives, even if the return this time was not after centuries, but after millennia.

Both projects, Liberia and Israel, share two features. Both brought the victim and the perpetrator together, around a common project. Supporters of Liberia included both white racists and their black victims, both former slave owners anxious to get rid of former slaves, and ex-slaves seeking refuge from a humiliating oppression. Similarly, the Israeli project has brought together both the Zionist right and the anti-Semitic Christian right. Secondly, both initiatives, Liberia and Israel, gelled around a civilizational project forged in the Diaspora. The Americo-Liberians were convinced that African natives needed to be civilized. They were also equally convinced that civilization was American, and they identified civilization with the green dollar as money, the top hat as the sign of a gentleman, and the white house as an appropriate residence for the country's president. For the Israeli Jew, a Palestinian is a squatter who must leave now that the rightful owner is back. Also for the Israeli Zionist, Israel is an outpost of Western civilization in the Middle East.

To return to my point, American cosmopolitanism is forged through a settler-colonial experience. It lacks sensitivity to native interests.

Let me conclude by suggesting a few issues for reflection. First, I suggest we reflect on the link between state terror and societal terror, such as the terror al-Qaeda unleashed on innocent victims in New York City on 9/11. My argument has been that societal terror, like that of al-Qaeda, was forged in an environment of impunity generated by state terror. This was true of the terror called 'black-on-black' or that called 'Nicaraguans-fighting-Nica-raguan' before 9/11, as it is true of what has been called 'Islamic terrorism' after 9/11.

Second, we need to reflect on the dramatic shift in US policy after 9/11. Before 9/11, the US counselled constructive engagement and reconciliation in the face of terrorism. These were code words for impunity and for sharing power. After 9/11, there has been a radical shift from calling for reconciliation to demanding justice, from total tolerance to zero tolerance. Justice is again a code word, for pursuing a vendetta and exacting revenge. The common ground between policy before and after 9/11 is that both ignore issues.

Here is my final suggestion for reflection. What is today called the War on Terrorism has two adversaries: the US and al Qaeda. Both came out of one side in the Late Cold War. One was nurtured by the other. Both use a political language marked by a strongly religious fervour. The point about religious language is that it is self-righteous It does not lend to compromise, for there can be no compromise between what is true and what is evil The righteousness of self goes alongside the demonization of the other as 'evil'. This kind of language tends to justify the use of power with impunity, and without accountability.

We are in a difficult situation, confronted by a double dilemma characterized by both state terrorism and societal terrorism. As we search for a solution, I suggest we remember the key lesson of the Vietnam War: do not conflate official America with the American people, or official Israel with the Israeli people. In the struggle ahead, in the struggle to hold power accountable, there is no force for peace and democracy more important than the very people in whose name that same power is being exercised today.

If American power is to police the world, then the peoples of the world have no choice but to hold American power accountable.

31

3

Léopold Sédar Senghor Lecture

Léopold Sédar Senghor: Senegalese Poet-President, 1906–2001

Fatou Sow

I am greatly honoured to give this lecture in honour of Léopold Sédar Senghor. Our generation of the independence years had mixed feelings about this President-Poet. He was a man of contrasts. Léopold Sédar Senghor was undoubtedly a state builder and ideologue. Since independence, after the very brief adventure of Mali federation with the former Sudan, he put in place all the institutions that form a state: the Constitution, an independent executive, judiciary and legislature, territorial administration, agrarian reform and even a family code which sought to place all the Senegalese communities under the same law, irrespective of their origin and religion. He set up an efficient diplomatic service held in high esteem not only in Africa but all over the world. He welcomed national liberation movements (PLO, PAIGC, ANC, SWAPO, etc.) and granted them diplomatic status. His political action was situated within the ideological framework of African socialism. Senghor was a highly respected member of Socialist International to which his party, the Socialist Party, is still affiliated.

However, we feel profoundly frustrated and even angry with Senghor, the politician. We have not forgiven him for leading Senegal in September 1958 to vote massively in favour of entry into a French-styled Commonwealth, against the no-less-massive 'No' vote of Sékou Touré's Guinea. In so doing, he isolated Guinea on the African political scene, taking with him a good number of his allies of the Rassemblement démocratique africain (RDA) [African Democratic Movement], a powerful party in the anti-colonial struggle in French-speaking West Africa. As President, he maintained Senegal in France's private preserve alongside Côte d'Ivoire and Gabon. His brand of socialism empowered the state which manipulated the masses more than it protected them from private French interests. He was President of a one-party state which he wanted to be strong; he closely controlled the peasant masses, through agricultural cooperatives, as well as academics, personally deciding who should be appointed to teach at the university. Thus, Cheikh Anta Diop, emeritus professor of Egyptology, was never allowed to teach at the university which bears his name, whereas he spent his entire career as a researcher there from 1956 to 1986. He rejected plans for a university program to teach African languages such as Wolof, Sereer, Pulaar, Mandeng, Hausa, Lingala, Swahili, etc., on an equal footing with French, English, Spanish or German and dismissed the promoter of the program, Pathé Diagne, the renowned Senegalese linguist. We are politely skeptical about his theory of Negritude considered to be different from, if not opposed to that of Aimé Césaire, author of *Cahiers d'un retour au pays natal* or that of Léon Gontran Damas, respectively his West Indian and Guyanese companions in the struggle in pre-war colonial France. Did Senghor not say that he relished 'the French language as he did jam' or again that 'emotion is Negro, reason is Greek'?

And yet, this man of culture won the admiration of his contemporaries. Holder of the agrégation in grammar (prestigious degree awarded by the French university), his academic and political career was exceptional on the then African political scene. Though sometimes loved, feared and detested by his peers, he was always admired. His poetry was touching. Who among us has not loved and recited 'Femme nue, femme noire', one of his most beautiful poems dedicated to the African woman?

Femme noire

Femme nue, femme noire
Vêtue de ta couleur qui est vie, de ta forme qui est beauté !
J'ai grandi à ton ombre ; la douceur de tes mains bandait mes yeux.
Et voilà qu'au cœur de l'Été et de Midi,
Je te découvre, Terre promise, du haut d'un col calciné
Et ta beauté me foudroie en plein cœur, comme l'éclair d'un aigle.

Femme nue, femme obscure
Fruit mûr à la chair ferme, sombres extases du vin noir,
Bouche qui fais lyrique ma bouche
Savane aux horizons purs, savane qui frémis aux caresses ferventes du Vent d'Est
Tamtam sculpté, tamtam tendu qui grondes sous les doigts du vainqueur
*   Ta voix grave de contralto est le chant spirituel de l'Aimée.*

Femme nue, femme obscure
Huile que ne ride nul souffle, huile calme aux flancs de l'athlète,
aux flancs des princes du Mali
Gazelle aux attaches célestes, les perles sont étoiles sur la nuit de ta peau
Délices des jeux de l'esprit, les reflets de l'or rouge sur ta peau qui se moire
a l'ombre de ta chevelure, s'éclaire mon angoisse aux soleils de tes yeux.

Femme nue, femme noire
Je chante ta beauté qui passe, forme que je fixe dans l'Éternel
Avant que le Destin jaloux ne te réduise en cendres pour nourrir les racines de la vie.

Léopold Sédar Senghor,
(Chants d'ombre, Éd. Du Seuil, Paris, 1959, pp. 15-16)

Black Woman

Naked woman, black woman
Clothed with your colour which is life, with your form which is beauty!
In your shadow I have grown up; the gentleness of your hands was laid over my eyes.
And now, high up on the sun-baked pass, at the heart of summer, at the heart of noon,
I come upon you, my Promised Land,
And your beauty strikes me to the heart like the flash of an eagle.

Naked woman, dark woman
Firm-fleshed ripe fruit, sombre raptures of black wine, mouth making lyrical my mouth
Savannah stretching to clear horizons, savannah shuddering beneath the East Wind's
eager caresses
Carved tom-tom, taut tom-tom, muttering under the Conqueror's fingers
Your solemn contralto voice is the spiritual song of the Beloved.

Naked woman, dark woman
Oil that no breath ruffles, calm oil on the athlete's flanks,
on the flanks of the Princes of Mali
Gazelle limbed in Paradise, pearls are stars on the night of your skin
Delights of the mind, the glinting of red gold against your watered skin
Under the shadow of your hair, my care is lightened
by the neighbouring suns of your eyes.

Naked woman, black woman,
I sing your beauty that passes, the form that I fix in the Eternal,
Before jealous Fate turn you to ashes to feed the roots of life.

Léopold Sédar Senghor, [Translated by John Reed and Clive Wake]

Our generation has been fascinated by this 'prolific' speaker. We participated in the numerous literary, philosophical, political and cultural debates he organized, making Dakar Black Africa's cultural capital. The Festival of Negro Arts brought together for the first time in Dakar in 1966 the whole of Africa and its Diaspora. I followed every minute of that magnificent event. And in view of Senghor's passion for the French language and his literary talents, he deserved his seat in the French Academy, after he left Senegal.

I cannot avoid saying a word about his relations with Cheikh Anta Diop, another exceptional intellectual. Cheikh Anta Diop was of course younger, but he and Senghor were contemporaries in political action and intellectual reflection. Although they did not have anything in common politically, and never confronted one another in an open debate, even on a non-academic platform, at least in Senegal, Léopold Sédar Senghor and Cheikh Anta Diop constantly dialogued with one another, answering, through their articles and works, each other's questions on Egypt, the cradle of humanity, on the precedence of African civilizations, on panafricanism, on the common heritage of African languages and many other debates I cannot open here. There was a certain intellectual rapport between them.

Senghor nevertheless left Senegal in ruins when he resigned in 1980, after ruling the country single-handedly for two decades. And yet, today many Senegalese miss the acumen and stature with which President Senghor imbued the State and its institutions. He firmly established the idea of *res publica*, i.e. the commonwealth, so vital in the face of the increasing informalisation of political power. It is obvious that his thought influenced an era of intense intellectual activity in the early years of post-colonial Africa dominated by his stature. He leaves an indelible mark in the history of our first years of independence.

4

Re-thinking African Development: And What if Women Had a Say in It!

Fatou Sow

Introduction

At the close of this 10th General Assembly of CODESRIA and this week during which we have made diagnoses, raised questions, voiced both doubts and convictions, some subjective, others objective, it would be an understatement to say that we all share one profound conviction.

At the turn of a new millennium, we live in a world in crisis, a world plagued by socio-economic and cultural upheavals that elude analysis and call for complex solutions. Such upheavals affect an economic order that has never been so dominated by market forces, a political order that weighs heavily on the state and on our systems of governance, corrupting relations between the state and the citizen. Never before has democracy and citizen participation been the subject of such intense debate, but what difference does it make, really? The systems to which states owe allegiance are shaped more by world market forces than by the demands of the popular masses whose votes are regularly sought.

'Development is dead, long live development!' one may proclaim, without trying to be witty. During the initial years of independence, well before this era of crises at the centre of our preoccupations, Léopold Sedar Senghor, first President of the Republic of Senegal, had promised his compatriots *natangué* (prosperity) with education and health for all by the Year 2000. René Dumont, the famous French agronomist, somewhat dampened the enthusiasm by writing as if in an outburst of anger that 'Black Africa got off on the wrong foot'. How many African intellectuals at the time did not protest against this early sign of Afro-pessimism that was in fashion in the 1990s. He was not taken seriously and the independence euphoria conjured up a miracle that never saw the light of day. The intellectuals also denied the Cameroonian essayist, Axelle Kabou, the right to ask herself the question 'And what if Africa rejected development?' Her essay, published in 1992, was a scandal in all African circles, from universities to political parties. And yet, the scale of the socio-economic and political disaster affecting the African masses described during our research compels us to re-think development and its rationale.

We are all jolted and challenged in our convictions by the fact that at the turn of this millennium, the major development priority on the continent is poverty reduction. With such a target, after forty years of independence and all sorts of development, cooperation policy and international assistance plans, how can we keep on raising the issue of the role of the African woman in development, a question which has been our primary preoccupation over the past two decades. The socio-economic situation is such that today, the Western media no longer focus so much on aid as on humanitarian work, which is the subject of sensational articles. For instance, in the area of health, the humanitarian assistance provided by Doctors Without Borders receives wider coverage in the media than cooperation agreements signed by Western states and Departments of Health. Some French students doing postgraduate diplomas or the MPhil. come to consult me in Paris 7 Denis Diderot where I spend a few months a year, requesting me to help provide them with justification for their specialization projects in humanitarian studies. They are utterly disappointed when I tell them I see no justification for such studies. They literally leave running when I sincerely discourage them from pursuing such studies, by showing them why neither generous humanitarian work nor cooperation can develop a country.

It is increasingly difficult, if not impossible for us to trumpet our feminist slogans of the 1970s and 1980s: participation, integration of women in the development process. Are we really rendering service to Africans by trying to integrate them in such development centred on poverty-reduction? Even our demand for gender equality in this complex context of abject poverty amid the continent's abounding wealth leaves us perplexed. At the international level, we have won several rights to equality whose enforcement our countries unfortunately cannot guarantee. We are obliged to refine our demands in the face of such development which needs to be re-thought by all the stakeholders. And yet...

We are the women and men of this continent and we consider ourselves ideological, theoretical and political allies until the gender issue puts us asunder, if it will not ultimately divide us. The gender issue, the question of relations between you and us cannot remain confined to disciplines reserved for women alone and to the field of women and feminist studies, which are marginal areas in the social sciences, both in the West and in Africa. We have been lucky, in our drive for the recognition of that discipline, its edification as a field of learning, and of policy and knowledge production, to have had some of you as allies. On the worldwide circuit of feminist conferences which I have been attending for the past two decades, I meet very few men, if at all any, whether in America, Europe or even Asia. Such conferences have remained a women's affair, which is not bad either, for this wards off a certain form of domination on the rostrum. At the last meeting on francophone feminist research, held in September 2002 at Toulouse-Le-Mirail University, France, my Western colleagues complained about the little echo their academic work was receiving from male colleagues. Such work nevertheless opens up extraordinary avenues for reflection and epistemological breaks in a large number of disciplines: sociology, psychology, literature, history and even philosophy, mathematics and the natural and medical sciences. I dare not ask this assembly how many men (and...women) are aware of the feministafrica website that our colleague, Amina Mama, has just opened, from the African Gender Institute she heads at the University of Cape Town, South Africa. I strongly recommend that you consult it and even contribute to it. I would also make the same recommendation to the women.

Three quarters of the students who attend my lectures on women, the family or feminist critique of the social sciences at Cheikh Anta Diop University, Dakar, are...men. This is in line with the 'natural' order of things, since girls represent only about 25 percent of the student population. Some of them also work on gender issues in any of their areas of study, much to the displeasure of my male colleagues who offer them more serious subjects.

We are forever indebted to Eboe Hutchful, Tiyambe Zeleza and Guy Mhone for being keen contributors and partners to the work *Engendering African Social Sciences* (it was not an easy step to take in the early 1990s), and to all those who emulated their example in other publications. The setting up of the Gender Institute marked a turning point in the institutionalization of that issue. It is our wish that other researchers (of both sexes) will make giant strides in integrating once and for all gender and social gender relations as essential aspects of our reflections and the management of the scientific and human resources of our institutions including this one.

My first question is: why this resistance?

Re-thinking Development in the Context of Globalization

The context in which we are invited to re-think development is that of globalization, which I will guard against defining before this august assembly of eminent experts. However, we know that this is not a new jargon coined by the international academic and political elites that we are. Globalization is indeed part and parcel of the everyday experiences of African people, including of course African women.

Housewives in the poor neighbourhoods of our African capitals or suburbs experience globalization on a daily basis. What is the relationship between Bouygues, a flagship French company, and a housewife in Pikine, Senegal? The housewife in that poor neighbourhood in the suburbs of Dakar queues up for long hours before the drinking fountain of her neighbourhood, sometimes far into the night or very early in the morning, to draw the water needed by her family. With the market liberalization policies of the 1990s, that foreign company (Bouygues) was entrusted with management of the water. Yet, independent Senegal acquired control of that resource only about ten years after independence, following tight negotiations with the private French firm that managed it during the colonial period. It should be noted that water is one of the rare natural resources that the French state has never succeeded in controlling institutionally, even in its own territory. In France, water is managed by three private firms, with some shares invariably held by the state. Water is a vital resource in a country's economy, as it meets the population's specific needs. In a few years to come, it will be a global economic and political resource. The interests of private companies do not necessarily tally with the concern for the wellbeing of poor families which cannot afford the exorbitant subscription charges exacted for services rendered by such companies. Any windfall from the Tobin Tax for financing development would significantly improve their lot.

Poverty has become a key word in development – poverty is a consequence of the collapse of states which are responsible for development. These states have claimed all the rights. Under the pretext of developing their people, they have perpetrated serious violations of democracy and human rights, freedom of expression and freedom to make public demands. Such states have not disentangled themselves from the web of corruption. Lopsided development has caused deep social divisions. Poverty is also a product of forty years of failed international aid and cooperation schemes blamed on state-guided development. The objectives targeted during decades of structural adjustment revolved mainly around the settlement of debts contracted by states which had to scale down their extravagant spending and social services, health and education budgets. Education and health are nevertheless productive sectors in which a country's work force is trained and supported. Education and health care are a vital investment in the local, national and regional economy. The draconian budget cuts have obliged African women to shoulder the greater part of all these services by virtue of the ideological conception of their reproductive capacities and usual domestic functions. Today, we cannot re-think development without taking into account the new challenges imposed by globalization. The changes on the global political landscape have reconfigured the context of development: end of the cold war, collapse of socialist systems, ascendancy of the neo-liberal economy, increase in American influence, civil and military conflicts worldwide, and particularly in Africa. Such conflicts in Africa, as elsewhere, are fanned by the thirst for political power to control resources.

During the 1960-1970 decade, Senegal and Côte d'Ivoire, a preserve of French influence, dialogued almost exclusively with metropolitan France. In 2000, at the Johannesburg Summit, Presidents Thabo Mbeki of South Africa, Abdel Aziz Bouteflika of Algeria, Olusegun Obasanjo of Nigeria and Abdoulaye Wade of Senegal, in a bid to jump-start NEPAD (New Partnership for African Development), had as counterparts, the G8 countries, the international institutions (World Bank, International Monetary Fund) as well as major private, semi-public, national and multinational companies angling for growth markets. This neo-liberal framework is a prerequisite for the negotiation of any trade agreement. Such a framework is an offshoot of political liberalism expressed in the common position adopted at the Summit, which was primarily in favour of democratization and democratic transition, good governance and transparency, even though the persons who enact laws are often embroiled in 'scandals' which show just how little they adhere to said principles.

The feminist research teams of the South which participated in the preparation of the work entitled *Marketisation of Governance* (2000), edited by Viviene Taylor,[1] (Aminata Diaw, Amina Mama, Charmaine Pereira and Ndri Assié-Lumumba wrote the chapters on Africa) discussed the dilemmas faced by the people on account of such a development rationale. Some of the most crucial of these dilemmas will be highlighted.

One of the first dilemmas identified is that of 'growth'. The exploitation and dependence created by market forces have an intolerable impact on the people. Growth is unstable and unemployment is on the rise. The woman's prime responsibility to feed the family has never been so heavy. Feeding the family is our 'natural' calling. The various crises have increasingly transformed women into heads of households, without granting them the legal status, political power and the other social, symbolic and cultural benefits that should go hand-in-hand with this de facto status.

'Political control' is another dilemma. The African state has been, rightly or wrongly, obliged to become a 'lesser state' institution. Does such a state still have control and regulatory power over its natural and economic resources? Such resources which include water, land, forests and the abundant mineral resources of the African sub-soil are increasingly the preserve of world institutions and mechanisms that compel African countries to open them up to the world market (liberalization, privatization). This creates enormous problems of sovereignty. The state becomes a 'commodity', just like the resources it is supposed to control. Whether we are dealing with the system instituted by a Mobutu-styled African dictator[2] whose personal wealth could reimburse the Zairian debt, or the open-market system, the DAWN feminists conclude that there is neither a philosophy nor a value system that allows for the redistribution of part of the wealth to those who have contributed to its production or to the destitute.

A third dilemma stems from the very production of wealth. The DAWN feminists are asking themselves what is the significance and value of work in today's neo-liberal context. From what point do women's household, agricultural and traditional activities become work? Marxists of course have ready-made definitions of work. What we also know is that our states and enterprises are increasingly incapable of providing work and a minimum subsistence wage to the people. There is an obvious increase in women's work and their household responsibilities, which is related to rising unemployment and the retrenchment of workers in the public and private sectors. Security and extravagant equipment often receive the lion's share in state budgets — that is, when the funds are not siphoned off for other ends. Civil conflicts are laying waste vital regions of the continent. Arms proliferation is at a record high on the continent, whereas what is needed is poverty reduction.

States that have succeeded in institutionalizing gender issues by enacting laws against sex discrimination and setting up services and programmes for women have not been able to deliver the goods. They are still making empty promises, such as curbing maternal mortality whose incidence is still very alarming, or giving women greater access to political power with a quota that is still too low to have any major political significance or impact. Never mind their claim that they are incapable of creating an enabling political and economic environment which guarantees the promotion of human rights, including women's rights, and institutionalizing gender equality to achieve social justice.

We share the positions taken on democracy, strengthening of the civil society, human rights and issues of freedom, economic and social justice. Nevertheless, political divisions will inevitably appear the moment we demonstrate how these challenges do not affect men and women in the same way. That is precisely where the debate between our male colleagues and allies ends. Analysis of the problem becomes more difficult. It is true that all women do not ascribe to our feminist analyses. Some of our comrades-in-arms desert us along the way. It is therefore imperative to shield ourselves from the facile criticism of borrowing, and even copying, wholesale, Western feminism or to fall in the trap of the 'off-the-peg mindset' against which I am put on guard by an excellent Algerian colleague and friend, a Senegalese at heart who, for years, has shared our struggles in Senegal and in Africa.

Re-thinking Development with Women: A Few Paradoxes of African Feminist Critique

The word 'feminist' is frightening in the university where I teach and in my Senegalese and Sahelian circles. I will often refer to the Sahelian region which is part of my cultural milieu. It is, nevertheless, important to find out how feminists go about the difficult task of re-thinking development. I cannot, at this juncture, open the debate on the concept itself, as its definitions have changed so much with time, policies and attitudes of the different protagonists of development. Let us consider it as a process, a blueprint for society, a platoon of power struggles, etc. Globalization adds a new dimension to it.

The 9th International AWID Forum on Women's Rights in Development, held from 3 to 6 October 2002, in Guadalajara, Mexico, had an ambitious theme: 'Re-inventing Globalization'. During a workshop organized in the fringe of the forum by DAWN, the network of feminist researchers/activists of the South, of which I am a member, we discussed several paradoxes encountered in our analyses and action strategies or in the work of other civil society or political protagonists.[3]

One of the first paradoxes is that of women's agency, an undoubtedly more apt expression which I have translated into French as 'la question ou l'agenda des femmes'. Today, we know from experience that we can no longer study women's agency per se. [Liberating women from the mould of socially constructed, disciplined and objectified beings] (G. Francisco), both on the private and public fronts, through our analyses and actions, is the crux of the matter. We also need to 'deconstruct' that which alienates women in the socially constructed identity of the woman, to 'deconstruct' social relations between men and women, which relations are still founded on the religion

43

and culture of inequality. The gender and inequality power struggles cannot be dissociated from other forms of power and inequalities based on class, caste, race, etc. We cannot dissociate this struggle from the struggle against all other forms of injustice.

We must also recognize the 'multi-centric' nature of the structures and relationships of power in various contexts—the family, the work environment, the state, other social realities—which are increasingly changing and becoming more complex. The challenges vary with the context, the history, the location and environment, hence the need for multiple solutions. By joining the struggle against the progressive forces, feminist critique has resolved many of the paradoxes.

Negotiating this struggle, 'negotiating gender', with men, political parties and civil society remains a longwinded and complicated process. Our joint organizations remain very male-dominated. Amina Mama, in her message at this conference, recalled the difficulties encountered in introducing, albeit implicitly, the feminine dimension of academic freedoms in the CODESRIA Kampala Declaration as recently as twelve years ago. We continue to encounter the same difficulties in all our commitments, whether public, academic or social. There have been so many discussions with a view to changing the term 'droits de l'homme' [which literally means 'rights of man'] into 'droits humains' [human rights] and to make our colleagues and political allies understand that 'droits de l'homme' do not encompass all the rights of women.

We collectively organized struggles against colonial and imperialist power, struggles against all forms of African dictatorships with a view to instituting a democracy which is neither transitional nor adapted to the African mindset, but a democracy of equality and justice. The struggles against globalization and other forms of globalization, the struggles against all forms of fundamentalism ranging from those espoused by George W. Bush and Osama Bin Laden to the return to authenticity championed by former Presidents Tombalbaye of Chad and Mobutu of Zaire, have galvanized us, men and women from all walks of life to protect rights to life and freedom. The oppression of women becomes intolerable in this context. And yet pursuing the debate right to the end to enable women to also benefit from the changes has been a herculean task.

Privatization policies on the natural, forestry or mineral resources market and the 'marketisation' of our states is a vital challenge and call to battle. But even in the thick of such battles, women are supposed to denounce, on the one hand, the patriarchal market, political and state policy orientations which curtail women's rights to citizenship and the freedom to exercise such rights, and the control exercised by wealthy men, on the other.

The problem of access to land does not only concern President Robert Mugabe. He is seizing land from white farmers who constitute 3 percent of the Zimbabwean population and occupy a majority of the most fertile lands, to give it to the Zimbabwean peasantry from whom the land was stolen by the apartheid regime. Yet how many women in the Zimbabwean peasantry have acquired land? The same question can be asked with regard to women of the River Senegal Valley where hundreds of thousands of hectares of irrigable land have been given out for cultivation. One of the major hurdles of the economy following the building of the dam is finding ways and means of developing the land: the male workforce is migrating to other countries. How many women have been considered as peasants and given land and agricultural equipment or loans? They invariably encounter the same difficulties of access as the poor peasant farmers of the Delta or the young single men obliged to form associations to prevent the elders from exploiting them. However, the cultural premises of access to land through marriage, the fact that the land can be withdrawn as a result of divorce or widowhood are issues raised only by feminists. It has taken a certain degree of state purposefulness and commitment to empower a handful of women to sit on rural communal councils which manage village land. Income-generating activities, so popular in the 1990s and on which women's NGOs thrived, succeeded in generating significant income from market garden produce. Whenever profits are substantial, plots and activities are ultimately withdrawn by the land owners, i.e., the husband, the relative, the village chief, etc. The same argument is raised to justify such seizures — that African land is communal and that usufruct rights take precedence, but even this right is restricted for women.

Recognizing the woman's right to have rights is a fundamental demand. It is constructive to criticize the concepts of good governance or democracy to which our states paid lip service during the periods of democratic transition. We objected to elections as mere window dressing since they were rigged. We nevertheless rejoiced whenever transparent elections resulted in democratic victories. Yet men become indignant when we argue that democratic rights also cover the right to control our bodies, our sexuality and our fertility; that the state and society should not be allowed to exploit us, nor to propose to us or withhold from us contraceptive methods, with a view to establishing a balance between population and resources. Female genital mutilation, a form of cultural labelling, does not only cause medical complications but, more important, inhibit women's libido and sexual pleasure. The right to sexual pleasure should not be reserved for the mistress or the prostitute, but it should also be enjoyed by the mother and the ordinary woman. We deliver in pain; can we not conceive in pleasure? The contracting of marriages with girls under the age of puberty, generally prohibited by family codes, is rape with impunity orchestrated by society. A few months ago, a little girl in a village in Eastern Senegal was withdrawn from school and married off to her cousin. She died a few days after her wedding night. Neither the marabout, nor the uncle, nor the members of the family that had arranged the marriage, in spite of her mother's refusal, were troubled by the local judicial authorities. RADDHO, a Senegalese human rights organization, had to cry foul in the media before the husband was incarcerated. He was hastily tried and sentenced to...two months imprisonment! We all know horror stories that are evidence of daily violations of women's rights: physical, sexual (rape, incest, forced marriages) and moral violence, etc.

I provoke the wrath of eminent colleagues the moment I assert at conferences that women should have the right to enjoy their sexuality and be impregnated by men of their choice, when they wish, in the setting they choose. I am simply stating the woman's right to choose her husband and the father of her children (as authorized by the family code which requires that marriage should be between consenting partners), not to become pregnant at too early or too advanced an age, given the health risks involved, etc. I was, however, accused of being unethical, of corrupting African moral values and plotting the demise of the African family. It is true that I demand the effective abolition of early and forced marriage, that I condemn forced sexual intercourse both in and out of marriage, that imposed on young girls under the pretext of protection from AIDS, sexual corruption by teachers, superiors, Sugar Daddies (known as Pa and demi-Pa in French-speaking Africa), gang rape of secondary school students by their mates of the same age group, rape in civil conflicts to humiliate other men, etc. All such acts of violence have been documented in feminist research.

Being a citizen is not a simple exercise for women. The fundamental freedoms, freedom of expression, movement and self-determination for the men and people dear to President Sékou Touré of Guinea are generally recognized, but why is there so much resistance to the same freedom of expression, freedom of movement and freedom of self-determination for women?

The right to practice a trade is a common trade union and political demand. However, it becomes problematic in the case of women, and for reasons that go beyond economic constraints. Although according to local traditions, women were only allowed to work in the agricultural, fisheries, local crafts and petty trade sectors, the Senegalese Family Code up till 1984 gave any man the right to stop his spouse from practising a trade. This right was granted to him as family head. Although that legal provision was ultimately expunged from the code, the one granting men the status of family head is still in force. It places the woman under the duty of obedience and submission. The husband exclusively has family authority and responsibility for the children, the power to determine the family's domicile, etc. Consequently, gainfully employed married women pay tax as single women with no children. They have no legal medical responsibility for their husbands and children and cannot take legal decisions on behalf of their children, etc. The husband is only divested of such authority in the event of death, or by a court order in case of divorce or declared incapacitation. In the family codes of some countries of the Maghreb, the woman is still considered a minor. However, those countries at least have a family code. Niger and Chad do not have one and Benin adopted its family code only in July 2002. In other countries, such as Mauritania, and in Northern Nigeria, the Sharia is practised.

Such constraints originate in cultural labelling and symbolic signifiers that vary, depending on whether you are a man or a woman. We also condemn the propagation of Western models and consumer goods on the markets of the South. Women are generally exploited by the major companies as managers of household consumption (household appliances, consumer goods). The woman's body is used as a sign post for marketing bouillon cubes, washing soap, cars, etc. This stripped body of the woman whose place is in the kitchen and whose primary calling is to bear children, is sold to the public. There is a cellular phone ad in which two posters are juxtaposed: one features a man wearing a tie (most probably a businessman) discussing with someone on the phone; in the other poster is a girl wearing jeans trousers chatting on the phone. Women absolutely must fight against such labelling and the use of their bodies by commercial and advertising firms as well as states for purposes of political fundamentalism, and by local companies as vehicles of cultural and religious fundamentalism. The labelling of the woman's body is the same; whether the woman is naked on walls or wearing a mini-skirt in the streets of Western capitals or wearing a veil in the streets of Kano, Mombasa or Algiers, her body is labelled in men's eyes. It must be exhibited or hidden from their gaze.

The state does not treat the woman as a full citizen. She is wife and mother protected, of course to make sure she properly carries out her reproductive function. Family codes, wherever they do exist, are contrary to constitutions

47

which all guarantee equal rights for all human beings without any distinction whatsoever. Yet those codes reek of discrimination. The state makes civil registration of marriages compulsory, passes legislation on polygamy, divorce, inheritance, alimony, as if it were protecting women from men's authority while reinforcing it at the same time. This supposedly 'natural' authority of men obliges us to question masculinity. Calling to question male domination in Africa is a perilous task; men are up in arms at the very idea. How can one seriously question male domination and highlight the patriarchal nature of political power, the state, the nation, state and judicial institutions and the international finance system in a debate as crucial as globalization of markets and policies? Women do not have the courage to take the bull by the horns whereas all the hallmarks of lopsided development are evident at every turn. Sometimes they even go as far as denying the existence of the gender problem. A number of female politicians assert that they owe nothing to the women's struggle. Alas!

Whenever I discuss the issue of violence against women in the family, in the school or professional environment or during conflicts, there is always a man who rises to his feet and bellows out that men are also battered…by women. Violence is already irrefutably rooted in family structures. The construction of the 'strong' man and the 'weak' woman is present in a good number of ideologies. The African family teaches the boy to lead and to take decisions, while girls are taught to be submissive and to obey orders. The woman's body is an object up for grabs. Matrimonial violence is almost 'justified'. Perpetrators thereof even have one mitigating circumstance in the case of the killing of a woman by her husband or partner, categorized as a crime of 'passion'. Acts of violence committed during civil conflicts occur in everyday life: assault, sexual abuse and rape. Women are raped by soldiers, police officers, rebels, etc. Today, the silence that has hitherto surrounded such acts of depravity is being broken even in Africa and in our more modest societies. Violence ultimately poses the problem of women's safety for which no measures are being taken. Security has become a priority in several states fighting domestic or international terrorism, armed robbery or urban crime. As a matter of fact, the Spaniards reported that in 2001 more women were murdered by their husband than by ETA.

Our societies, by and large fall under patriarchal and matrilineal systems more than matriarchy. The handing down of political power or property by women is a system that has been described in all its aspects by ethnologists. Such systems, for the most part, are dual. The introduction of the religions of the Book (Islam and Christianity) and of the colonial cultures have altered the value and reference systems, sometimes profoundly adulterating them, hence the numerous contemporary demands for constitutional recognition. However, we cannot return to the 'authentic' culture without first questioning it. Culture re-introduces the age, gender and caste systems that fashion societal inequalities. The return to authenticity is more problematic for us than for the men who 'flirt' with the discourse of authenticity under the guise of modernity or authenticity. They can conveniently leave it or return to it. We, who have been delegated to be 'custodians' of culture, do not enjoy such flexibility. Religion becomes a problem when it is used as a means of acceding to political power and not as a faith system. I take Islam as an example — and without any complex — since I am of the Muslim culture. Over the past months, I have not stopped wondering how come Islam passes for a culture of terrorism. Between Bush, Bin Laden and their respective fundamentalist positions, Amina Lawal's death sentence for 'fornication' and the turbulent election of Miss World in Nigeria, I no longer have the time to present the results of research on women, law and Islam in Senegal. I have difficulty reasoning with counterparts who want me to take a stance either for or against Islam. Yet, several participants here, living in Africa, are from a Muslim or Christian cultural background which, in any case, is religious. Whatever may be their level of belief, practice or indifference, they are affected by the current environment to which we all belong. I personally view Islam as a religion of appeasement. It saves me many metaphysical anxieties. I do not have to try to understand how Mohammed is the Son of God (he is only his messenger) or the mystery of the Virgin Mary, Mother of God. When I sin or need moral consolation, I can always turn to God, without any human intermediary. To Souleymane Bachir Diagne, author of 'Cents mots pour comprendre Islam' [One Hundred Words to Understand Islam], I must say I need much less to understand Islam, or at least to understand what I need in Islam for my religious practice.

Islam has consistently been exploited for political ends, which makes debate on the subject in Africa difficult. Religion is as much a faith as an instrument for conquering power. From the Almoravides to El Haj Umar El Fuutiyu, the Jihad has been an instrument for conquering political power and land. Islam has also been an instrument of popular resistance and recognition in the face of colonial power and its institutions. The British, as a general rule, left local political systems such as the sultanate and the Almamia intact, although they corrupted the leaders and put them at each other's throats, whereas the French, by and large, abolished them. Muslim fraternities emerged or were reinforced, resuming the local political tradition, e.g., the

49

Tidiane, Mouride, Layeen or Khadir fraternities in Senegal. We can cite many other cases elsewhere in Africa. The advantage a country like Senegal has is that a century of French colonization has impregnated our legal and political heritage with secularism. Reference is never made to the Sharia, except in the family code which governs relations between men and women. It is obvious that against this backdrop, the Islamic question cannot affect us in the same way.

The question of Islam and politics in Africa revolves around the power struggle among Islamic groups. Discussions here will focus on the Iranian Revolution of the 1980s; the action of the FIS and the GIA in Algeria; the civil war in Sudan which has pitted Muslims against Christians for the past thirty years ; the islamization/arabization of political power in Mauritania, instituted by the Maures (to their advantage), against the other Hal Pulaar communities, the Soninke and the Wolof of the Delta region and the River Senegal Valley ; the use of the Sharia in the States of Northern Nigeria against the Federal Government; the conflict in Côte d'Ivoire between the Christian Akan South and the Muslim Mandeng North; the formation of cultural, political and economic Muslim elites; the mysteries of science revealed in the Koran; the Koran's compatibility with development, etc.

Both the general public and scholars are fascinated by such debates. The Senegalese were shocked to see President Wade, accompanied by his Government, prostrating themselves before his Mouride marabout, after his victory in the 2000 presidential elections and the 2001 legislative elections. They condemn the growing interference of clerics in politics. However, it took about twenty years for doctors to admit and to accept to say in Muslim circles that excision was sexual mutilation, harmful to women's health. When the family code abolished the husband's right to object to his wife's employment, journalists (young men) raised a general outcry against that measure. It is scandalous that all that states have retained from the Sharia are the provisions regarding the individual status of women which oppress women by making them subservient to men. Polygamy, the powers endowed on husbands and fathers and the wearing of the veil are the subject of very heated debates. Do we respect human rights by condemning Sadiya Husseini and Amina Lawal for fornication, imposing the fatwa on journalists like the Chadian, Zahra Yacoub, for producing a documentary on excision, or on the Nigerian, Isioma Daniel, for writing that the Prophet could have married one of the contenders in the Miss World contest? Nigerian feminist organizations condemned Isioma Daniel's article, but they also denounced the fatwa as unlawful. Many of my male colleagues assert that the Sharia is part of our Muslim culture and that we should adapt to it. It is difficult to engage in a legal, political or scientific debate on areas of application of the Sharia, for they uphold men's power. Secularism is observed everywhere, save in this area. We must dismiss those who manipulate religion for political ends, whatever may be their platform.

This raises a crucial philosophical and political question: How do we separate religion from politics?

Conclusion

Pursuing the debate at several levels is a priority, if we are to effect positive change in gender relations. Our area of research is no exception to the rule. Imposing roles and relations between the sexes as a variable in the analysis of all situations is indispensable to building a society based on equality and social justice. During the International Association for Women's Rights in Development (AWID) forum held in Guadalajara in October 2002, women tried 'to imagine a world without poverty, without violence and discrimination; a world in which each person's needs are satisfied and human rights are protected; a world in which women's rights are both a means and an end of development'. In the same vein, at the close of this forum, I would like us all, dear colleagues, to proclaim: 'You want to globalize: globalize this, therefore: the rights of women in development!'

Notes

1. The French version was edited under the title: *Marchandisation de la gouvernance*, by Fatou Sow, DAWN Coordinator for French-speaking Africa.
2. Former President of Zaïre.
3. Workshop with Peggy Antrobus from Barbados, Gigi Francisco from the Philippines, Viviene Taylor from South Africa, Sonia Correa from Brazil and myself from Senegal.

www.ingramcontent.com/pod-product-compliance
Lightning Source LLC
Chambersburg PA
CBHW031448280326
41927CB00037B/398